One Hungry Baby

ORCHARD BOOKS
96 Leonard Street, London EC2A 4RH
Orchard Books Australia
14 Mars Road, Lane Cove, NSW 2066
ISBN 1 85213 374 0 (hardback)
ISBN 1 85213 498 4 (paperback)
First published in Great Britain 1992
First paperback publication 1993
Text copyright © Lucy Coats 1992
Illustrations copyright © Sue Hellard 1992

Printed in Belgium

With much love for A.J.C. and P.E.C.
who led the way.
For J.R.O. who gave me the time.
And for Archie,
my very own hungry baby.
L.M.O.

One Hungry Baby

A Bedtime Counting Rhyme

Rhyme by
Lucy Coats
Pictures by
Sue Hellard

ORCHARD BOOKS

One hungry baby

Three dribbly chins
With bibs underneath.

Four bubbly bathtimes
To wash off the crumbs.

Five sploshy splashers

Five wet Mums.

Six funny Dads
Drying six button noses,

Seven big sisters
Counting tails and toeses.

Eight fat teddies

Ready for bed

Nine soft pillows,
Nine sleepy heads.

Ten good babies Tucked up tight.

Twenty tired parents
Waving good night.